Mineral Miracles

Lucy Fenton

BookLeaf
Publishing

India | USA | UK

Presentation by *BookLeaf Publishing*

Web: www.bookleafpub.com

E-mail: info@bookleafpub.com

ISBN: 9789360948443

First edition 2024

*To my mum, my dad and my brother for
their endless love and support.*

And to myself. I did it.

ACKNOWLEDGEMENT

I would like to acknowledge my most favourite poet Billy Collins whose poetry and ability to make meaning from the most innocuous of places unlocked something in me when I was a teenager.

I would also like to acknowledge various poets from DeviantArt, too many accounts to name and usernames long since forgotten, but those poets and that website fostered my fledgling creativity and allowed me to experiment with a variety of poetry styles.

It goes without saying but I will say it anyway: thank you to my mum and my dad and my brother, Sam, who have always championed me, supported me through countless struggles, picked me up when I've been down and always set me straight. I love you all so, so much and cannot thank you enough for all you do for me.

Thank you to BookLeaf Publishing for giving this opportunity to aspiring writers like myself. Because of you, I can call myself a published poet!

Thank you Tom for all you do for me. I love you.

And finally, thank you to myself for getting through the hard days, for giving myself grace when life throws unexpected curveballs, and for conquering my ADHD long enough to get this collection together. I finally feel like my mind and I are a team at last and this anthology, my mineral miracle, is proof of that.

PREFACE

When putting together this anthology, I knew I wanted to use the phrase 'mineral miracles' from my poem 'Seventy percent water' as the title. To me, it perfectly encapsulates what this anthology is: the literary equivalent of closing your eyes and sticking a hand into a mixed assortment of rocks and crystals. You don't quite know what you're going to get. To some, the poems might be chalky and hard and incongruous with one another. They don't have straight edges and perhaps don't fit together in perfect, orderly lines. But, to others, the poems might glitter when you catch them in the light at just the right angle. They might have sparkling quartz veins and look like beautiful obelisks on your bookshelf.

These poems were written over the course of my teenage years and my twenties, all the way up to the age of 29 (my current age as of publication). Some of my work is new ('The rat in the flowerpot' was inspired by the death of my pet rat Remus in January 2024, the first pet I'd ever had all to myself who was solely reliant on me and sadly died of a pituitary tumour). Some of my work is older ('Graveyard shift' was written in 2015 in the midst of my experience as a university student battling undiagnosed ADHD and struggling to keep up with the demands of my course). Some of my work is what I would consider to be more 'traditional' poetry ('i. The divide', 'ii. The loss', 'iii. The reunion') while other poems are more experimental in nature ('Battery' comments on the experience of battery hens and industrial farming inspired by Les Murray's 'Pigs').

Although these poems were written from different places and for different purposes (my university course, expressing teenage angst, my own entertainment, etc), I hope my mineral miracles can reach out to you from the page and, regardless of their reader's background or experience, can resonate with you in some small way.

Seventy percent water

What do they do with the half-finished people?
The ones hydrating in the womb
for nine long months,
only to be born as still and cold
as the surface of a pond.

Half-finished people whose star signs
did not have time to swim
the whole of the universe.
A Pisces dies of cancer, a half-finished
person, blood running
with chemical agents – a whole lake
full of upturned fish.

The unfinished food of half-finished people
lost to the murky depths of toilet bowls
before it can spread like a smooth
duvet over half-formed ribs.
They drink nutrients from IV drips
and die with thick river silt in their lungs.

Sometimes, half-finished people go to school.
Or cafés and theatres. Or walk the streets.
Then, like the split-second of a tsunami,
are washed away in a hail of bullets and IEDs.

We see them again in the pearl drops of tears
and gather up their oyster shell bodies
for processing.

I like to think half-finished people are recycled
into clean drinking water.
They dance through Brita filters,
warm themselves in the bath –
mineral miracles that hold hands across the earth
and free-fall in the rain.
They fill jars of sea monkeys and look back
when half-finished people,
older and younger than themselves,
tap on the glass.

For the sake of the bodies

I thought at first
they kept the exhibition cold
for the sake of the bodies.
In the cool, air-conditioned dark
of the warehouse of human corpses,
I expected to scream
- or faint. Instead,
it turned me inside out.

I didn't realise until after
that what I had walked round
was a cemetery
dressed up as a museum.
Glass cases for coffins, specimen jars for urns.
Instead of earthworms chewing flesh
into carbon,
silicon and formaldehyde
clung to the preserves of bones.
Compressed every aspect
of what it meant to be human;
more polyepoxide than person.

While there, I saw arthritic fingers, dirt
still trapped under the nails,
gnarled as though they'd been

banging against a coffin lid for hours.
A woman with no head, but still implanted
with her intrauterine device;
even dissected
still railing against
the roots of the seed of life.

From frames, central nervous systems hung
like shaggy Halloween cobwebs.
A brain shot through
with bubbles of blood. I thought
of the skull it had been in,
of the person he was.
And pondered how many lives that
one haemorrhage had touched.

Smokers' lungs were suspended in chambers -
sick and fat, heavy with tar.
Staring at them made me wheeze.
Next to them was a collection box
full of cigarettes.
I wondered how many people left theirs
behind and how many went out later
to buy more,
cursing themselves all the while.

The best display
was the most unremarkable.
Simply a cross-section of a human,

a sliver of life, turned on her side.
The skin was an inch deep,
slabs of kidneys and veins
perfectly preserved in a long torso.
The plaque next to her
didn't have anything special to say,
just listed the parts that were there
like a shopping list.

But when I tilted my head to the right,
crouched on my knees,
I could see the pale bridge of her nose.
Her head was shaved but up close,
I saw fine hairs glistening
above her upper lip.
Dust had gathered on the ends of her eyelashes.
Her glass eye looked out at me
from between hooded lids.

I forgot all the science under that passive
gaze, silently asked her
her name. I tried to imagine
what she had looked
like whole.
But that slice of flesh was cut too thinly
for me to see anyone's face
but my own.

King of the Forest

The deer are awake when a car cuts through the
forest,
their lamp-eyes expanding and contracting to the
flicker of
Xenon headlights, a passing camera flash against
the infinity of the trees.

The air gnaws at spindly legs with its icy teeth.
A herd of deer moves over the earth in a brown
flush,
mindless but for the hot rush of mates and the
scarlet scent of dogs.
Tyres squeal in the darkness. White ears flick up.
Hunters are sprinting through the forest
on a black road running like a river of oil.
The stink of petroleum and fire alights wet
nostrils.

Hearing the anxious snorts of the herd mothers,
deer through time come alive. From cave walls,
Irish elk
step out of the stone, cloven hooves scraping the
wet mud.
Black flanks peel as the charcoal paint rustles to
life.

Tiny Cretan deer with spatula antlers, daubed in
ochre,
spring up from the ground and weave between
wobbly, two-dimensional legs.

Fallows and roes blur, tucked beneath their
ancestors.
Repeated pairs of yellow discs are the eyes of all
deer,
staring out from the refuge of the forest.
Sloping shoulders quiver, searching for silver
spears
parting the leaves. In tandem, deer snouts brush
the forest floor and wait,
antlers toppled like gilded crowns.

As the breaths of the forest quiet with the
passing of moonlight
beacons and the fading roar of an engine,
one deer can feel all of his genus pulsing behind.
He fears no rivals in this glorious age, his bone
wreath lopsided
but well-fought and won. This buck is no
stranger to predators:
his head is mounted in a thousand log cabins. He
remembers
what was once the slow bleed-to-death of arrows
or the shock of clubs.

The stag lays his head on the verge, thankful for
the sudden mercy
of speeding cars.

The rat in the flowerpot

I picked a sunflower
to grow around him,
that tiny, black and white
star, so wrinkled
by the end, hairless
and collapsing
from the inside.

A sunflower, bright
yellow like his aura,
holding warm sunlight
made of four paws
and a long, curling
tail that the earthworms
mistake for a spiralling
tendril of the galaxy.

Yes, a sunflower,
golden lucky charm
smiling back at the
burning fire in the centre
of the solar system.
Do his round ears
act as satellites?

I hope when the bees
have gone and the petals fall,
he is carried away on the breeze
that drags the summer
back home to autumn.

I hope on that wind,
he bursts through white
clouds, goes high into space,
sniffs at the sun with
his pink nose and whiskers.
I hope it reminds him
of home.

If we won the lottery

We would keep our childhood home, we agreed.
The 2-bed-that-became-a-3-bed bungalow.

We lived life in one storey, foundations of the house
spreading like a map.

There's a crack in the living room ceiling that always came back,
despite multiple replasterings and splashes of paint.

The big bedroom my brother and I shared; we built a fort—
really a tunnel, two duvets spread across the chasm between our beds.

He's a police officer now in London and I still feel that duvet bridge,
connection in every text message I send: "Get home safe."

The driveway wasn't long enough for all our cars,

I wondered if the neighbours minded as we
sprawled out across the street.

Or the way our dogs bark back and forth at each
other through time.
The ginger cat watches the new black and white
one, his yellow eyes slitted.

In the garden now, there's a little solar fountain
that trickles when the sun hits
just right. You can hear it under the notes of my
dad's piano,

songs rising through the glass window like
branches of trees
planting themselves in the air, the atmosphere
around our house.

Back inside and my mum is making a cup of tea.
The mugs change colour
a thousand times. Her taste is the immaculate
taste of mothers

making bricks and mortar into a home, a flat
palace fit for her family.
Yes, we agree, if we won the lottery, we would
keep that extraordinary bungalow,

a museum all for ourselves where a whole
universe could come to visit
and walk away having learned the meaning of
warmth,

a church where every living breathing thing
could step inside and feel the higher power of
what it means to love.

On visiting the canal boat in the middle of the night one freezing cold January/I want to quit my job

There's a poem in the way
my dad rushed out at 3am to travel 2 and a half
hours
north to his canal boat
freezing out in the marina.

The dog's water bowl was iced over,
breath blowing like smoke from hot coals.
The urgency of his gloved fingers,
spilling water from the boiler and replacing it
with anti-freeze. It's a sigh—

set free on the frozen canal, the black moon
a penny shimmering above,
cloudless air letting all the sound out.

The poem came in the car later,
him driving home anonymously,
me on the phone to my mum and her telling
this tale of sudden adventure, flared by panic,

an unsettled night driving a man to action
like a locomotive chugging steam,
restless and forward until forced
to turn around.

The poem was me, laughing—
the realisation both a slap to the face
and the salve after:
"That's where I get it from!"
as my life's pendulum
starts to fall back
in the other direction.

Overthinking

I held the first idea in my hands,
but the other one,
it had legs.

It ran – sprinting and hollering,
an unexpected child into the path
of a car, clutching
a teddy in one hand,
its mother's promises
in the other.

Luckily, another one had legs.
It ran – loping and silent.
I chased it halfway around the globe,
waited in soot, among clothes pegged out
on washing lines, in the snow.
By the time, it circled back to me
it was like catching light.

Then came a few, in quick succession,
four-legged and frenetic.
They ran – playful and comforting.
Too safe, like familial laughter,
like finding the crease
of a creaky floorboard.

I shut the window on them,
empty-handed. I went to bed,
and the last idea opened the door
in the middle of the night. It had legs.
It walked – soft and barefoot
over threadbare carpet,
settled into wait until I found it
in the morning, a jigsaw of dust motes
drifting in my mind.

The railway children

Sorry for arriving late on the train to life,
I made you wait
and waiting you stood, clad in grey.
You were faceless among cherry blossoms of red
that day.

The train pulled in at 12 o'clock,
but I don't know if that's midnight or midday
anymore.
This journey has taken an ice age.
Those Catholic oil-painting clouds have
forgotten my name,
and I'd say I mind but really I don't,
because you still waited for my train
all the same.

For one moment there, I swear we chugged
through ponds of weeds and dragonflies
and I caught one and pulled off its wings,
grounded it to a crane fly state,
then spat it back up in life's careless face,
and still this pathetic train chugged on,
at a thousand miles an hour
into the sun.

Occasionally I could feel lava
eating at the metal of this carriage and
I wasn't scared -
I promise I wasn't.
Because, through the clouds of smoke and
steam,
you were still running faithfully
beside me through that clogged carriage
window,
waving handkerchiefs at the driver.

And when I finally pulled into life,
there you were, sweat-stained, ash-grey,
sooty and sweet on the saffron platform line,
where together we jumped over
onto those electric tracks
and traversed the veins of earth,
hand in hand,
marvelling time.

Graveyard shift

18/11/15

Michael Caine said one time,
"you ain't got nothing
if you ain't got your peace of mind"
or something to that effect.

And goddamn me but I think it's true,
my soul is dried out like
some post-apocalyptic Louvre,
as if the paintings have been scrapped
for firewood. Glass pyramid, a relic
to the eons gone by. I see
a bitter Mona Lisa in my own eyes.

I'm aged now, lived a thousand years in twenty,
but above all I know I'm too old
to be so impatient, to know so little,
so not cut out for this game of life.
One day my grave will read
"Here lies a millennial"
and everyone who sees it will understand.

In another future, where we cross stars,
leave me on Mars where flowers

don't grow. I'd like to lay back in the dust,
feel the weak warm sun, taste red earth
on my tongue. That Rover and I could
keep ourselves entertained
for hours. I'd relish in a planet
that's already ended.

There's too much beginning on Earth
for my taste, my mind won't keep up.
I'm wide awake, am not at peace and
I can't rest with all this noise.

Morning shift

10/02/24

Jodi Foster said one time,
"we belong to something
that is greater than ourselves" and
"that none of us are alone!"

And thank God but I think it's true,
I came home from war
several years ago and in the
battlefields of my soul,
flowers grow. Winding paths
carve through meadows
where grasses brush past the top of my hip
and an abundance of butterflies
fill the air.

Mona Lisa is smiling again.
I'm even older and, above all,
relishing the sweet passing of time.
What a blessing it is to get to age,
to feel the universe looking out for
my soul's home, closing windows
when it rains and opening doors
when I least expect it.

One day, my grave will read something
that is not my business
but I hope it speaks of love
and that everyone who sees it
will understand.

In this future, I stay on my home planet.
I plant my little garden meadow,
lay back on the grass,
feel the sun and taste life
on my tongue.

There's too much beginning on Earth
and how wonderful it is, I'll take what I like,
leave the rest. I'm wide awake,
brimming with peace and
I sing along at the top of my voice.

Cocobello

The beach is crowded with holidaymakers.
The sand isn't quite the tropical white of the
Caribbean –
instead, it's an oatmeal shade,
the colour of dust in Roman ruins.
The water laps at the shoreline in tiny kitten
licks,
sandpaper-salt tongue edging ever nearer
to the optimistic towels laid down hours ago,
when the horizon was further away.

It's a dance, quickstep, watching sun
worshippers
struggle for the shoreline. They abandoned
their sandals in the pine forest behind,
now the sand bites at their toes.
Flies scatter as they polka past the line
of sea debris. In the distance, the shaded cafe
is a reprieve from the sun's energy. People top
themselves up
with iced drinks, plates of fries and shots of
caffeine.
Languages are shouted thunderously,
as if volume can breach borders.

Weaving between the leisure are the
beach sellers, laden with fake tattoos and towels.
Young girls have their hair braided,
feel like warrior princesses and can tell their
friends
in coloured string exactly where they've been on
holiday.
Knock-off watches, knock-off bags, knock-off
jewellery
clanks and clatters in portable cabinets,
laying tracks along the beach. The fluffy towels
of the finest Egyptian cotton will last a lifetime.

Lastly comes the coconut man.
From a bucket of water, lined with net, he hands
out
slices of coconut. It's expensive - 1 euro for a
slice of coconut
you could get whole for 75 cents
in the supermarket two kilometres away.
His voice announces his coming,
loud call of "Coco Bello, Bello, Bello!"

I buy a piece to take with me as we crawl back
up the beach
with the fading of the sun. It tastes like nothing,
like holiday air sweetened by joy. When it slips
from my hands,
lands in cooling sand, I shrug and we all laugh,

bemoan the waste. I'd go back and get another,
but he's too far now, the cry of "Coco Bello!"
disappearing up the coastline and fading away.

The one who writes

I meet in the café on the corner
with myselves from alternate universes.

It's good to catch up every now and then
with the one of me with two kids and a
mortgage.
These chats are a bit of a break, she always says,
restless and checking her watch.

The one who went to war six years ago
is looking better, we agree. Her eyes
focus now, jump less at the edges.
She's supremely amused by another me,
relearning gravity after a stint on the ISS,
mindlessly tossing spoons into the air.

These selves are pragmatic, practical.
They clash with my other girls;
the hippy who went to Italy on the promise
of a brochure and a smile,
the cartoonist who eats out of tins,
on the weekends paints placards of arses and
arrows,
and the faith preacher who's licensed
for a spot by the fountain,

an upturned hat at her feet
as she screams into the void.

I mostly observe. Even in my own universe,
I'm the quietest of us. The one who struggles to
speak
to customers in a crappy nine-till-five
and whose eyes water when hit hard
enough by fluorescent lights.

Meanwhile, the politician of me thinks
it's her job to stick up for me
in conversation, asking
about my notebooks in the same tone I use
to a customer who can't pay.

We natter awhile, going round in circles,
drinking green tea from teapots mostly,
the occasional biscuit. One of me likes coffee
and it's a shock to us all.
At last, the sun begins to dip
and we pack up. Long way home,
we joke, same as ever.

I watch them all go, the last to leave.
They saunter, strut, and shuffle off
in equal measure. In every passerby,
I can see all their selves. The heroes and the
crooks,

the loud ones and the silent ones,
miming for loose change.
I take it all in and try to jot it down,
like some kind of poet.

Nocturnal Animal

I wrote yet another poem
but this one was alive.

The first was the passion project
of a teenager pretending to be in violent love.

The second was the hatched shell
of a new adult who stood trembling,
with wide-eyed and bent legs, peering around
at the mess of her twenties.

This one comes like a nocturnal animal.
She is purposeful, proud,
carries words in her mouth like carrion…

They are not the juiciest cuts of meat
but she has learned to be resourceful.

Her words are sparing—
she has been hit by cars before,
blinded by beams of light that she believed
were salvation.
Her tail is crooked now,
a toothed half-smile
glints in the darkness.

She limps when it's cold

and chooses the cover of darkness,
audienceless as she prowls the dangerous
neighbourhood of my mind.

Sometimes she chooses to sit on the fence
and chirp at the moon,
sometimes she picks the wrong house
and passes the night shaking beneath the
cupboard.

My favourite nights are the ones she spends with
me—
little by little, I am coaxing her in
slowly, slowly, she is learning
to prefer the warmth of a soft bed.

She curls in the blankets
and finds the purr in her throat in time to the
hum of my finally-quiet mind.

Everest

I began
a mound of rock
under the sea,

pushing up over centuries.
The growth spurt
of earthquakes

raising me by degrees,
thousands of years
and I breach the waves, crowning

a steadily rising peak,
glaciers unfurling like wings
around me. Ice running slick, fault lines,

flat ridges, coarse edges.
Magma churning in the belly of the Earth.
I breathe new air, catch up to the necks of
sauropods,

pterodactyls fly about my head.
I watch them crash at the coming of meteors, the
burst

of volcanoes, see the sun disappear behind
sulphate aerosols,

carbon clouds unfold like parasols, wide open.
I pull everything into my stone flesh, gestate
calcite and limestone,
schist and quartz. Overtake trees at my feet as
India pushes northward into EuroAsia—

when finally the cliff face sheers off, my plateau
reached
at the bend of the horizon, the winds of the jet
stream carrying climbers away.
I don't look down. I taper my gaze on the points
of stars and try to reach the summit of space.

Battery

Brood balance on wire dirt, does brood.
Feathers plucked, thousand toes,
brood's sideways eyes rove.
Combs bent over, sickly pink
the colour of brother-pigs,
squealing in the dark.
Us the brood watch eggs pass,
no clutch of young brood,
our empty womb. Air is rotten.
Stench of poultry. Eggs, eggs, eggs.
Always eggs. Brood pecks,
eat ourselves the brood, tight press,
three to a cage. Feed funnelled
through pipes, snapping beaks,
chemical seeds. When bird flu
comes, gas filters in.
Flightless wings, brood sings,
cluck, cluck, cluck. And us brood
who've never seen the sky-yolk,
still crow. We brood cackle
when farmers take our necks
and twist our heads back,
like weathervanes.

i. The divide

My muse had to split. It caught
the hovercraft to the Isle of Wight.

I sat on pebbles at Southsea beach,
watched it go in a wash of bubbles and sea foam.

The Americas Cup was on, flags flickering
on the horizon like unnamed flyers

pinned against a graffiti sky,
all mottled purples and fierce browns.

I said, "I think it'll rain". "No time," you huffed.
Looked at your watch. "Better get back."

Then, a jolt in my veins, the call of boredom,
an ache. Its centrepoint was you.

I said, "good idea, I'm tired." Across the bay,
felt my muse crinkle and die, like a wave.

ii. The loss

I followed the underwater current
to West Wittering beach.

For the longest time, I counted hours
in the grains of sand. By the water's edge—

that shimmering graveyard—I could hear
most clearly the echoes of my muse.

It sang like a siren, ordering me to the deep.
I would've gone. But for the fact you came,

unhurried, a loping tide. You were sympathetic
like an iceberg, cold hand in mine.

"Something will come to you," you said.
Walked on. I stared at you as driftwood, a piece.

It was the end but still. I wanted posters put up.
Missing: my muse. Lost at sea.

iii. The reunion

The Needles brooked no argument. They cut
the horizon like shark fins, let the sky run open,

unchecked. I'd been hollow for months,
a shipwreck at the mercy of your tidal moods.

I needed a break. Something in the air, a catch
of salt and brine. Cuttlebone on the beach.

Somehow, the Solent was as still as a lake,
the winter air carrying on it the breath of

Arctic explorers. You were miles away,
trapped in a phone, a message in a bottle.

Heard myself say, "I'm done". Cut you off.
I left your protests in the cries of gulls behind.

Inside, all at once, chalk cliff faces cracked.
And I felt my muse come flooding back.

Vision of the Future

I hold a funeral in the garden.
My hands clench the empty shoebox—
no hamsters or ashes to be had.
My congregation is daffodils,
yellow faces downturned by the wind.
How is it spring already?
There I go again…
I'm wandering away. It's the reason
I'm here. I steel myself to bury
every version of me,
past present.
Future inhabits my body.
She let herself in when I turned 28.
She is fickle and free, callous and destructive
as she draws on the walls inside my mind.
She's just excited—puts up photos
of non-existent, nebulous infants,
screenshots of my growing Instagram crowd,
posters of the film of the book I've yet to write,
money notes stapled to plaster.
The box in my hands rattles.
The small garden is stifling
but the sky above is so wide.
"Put me back," something pleads in my palms.
"Calm down," I beg her.

The voice in my head is nervous laughter.
It's already getting late.
"There's time, there's time, there's time."

Citronella

Tonight is a yellow night, a roaring night.
If nights were lions, this one hunts the sun from
the sky,
pulls it to the dusky beach and rips at golden fur,
shaking the sand from its teeth. We scatter

nervous energy. Around both wrists, we wear
glow sticks
and they flash in sequence, fireflies alight
with warnings and promise. The air is rich with
fruit
and peeling skin and we wait to feast on life.

In the dark, a match is struck. With the
fireworks,
we light up. The moon swells over the sea, bitten
persimmon,
and we raise our hands when the music starts,
communicate like cicadas through twined legs.

Around the carcass of the sun festering in
this yellow night, we flock like flies. We breathe
through our mouths, taste amber smoke and
beer,

and the whip of salt at the back of foreign
tongues.

To the beat of tealights in plastic cups, we dance.
Like mosquitoes, we tremble until the ultraviolet
of dawn.
We throb in electric spasms, a scourge,
our bodies pulsing with a blood not our own.

I've started writing again

42

The first pencil stroke—
pencil, because it's erasable,
illegible if left alone long enough—
is breathlessly quiet,
a fox cub taking
its first tentative steps
on the snow.

SNAP! The pencil breaks and
it shocks me, the heartbeat
flash of anxiety, my tender foe.
I am stripping the fear out
of its spoiled clothes.
I lay it down like
an infant on the page,
legs aloft, waiting for change.

A smile streaks my lips
as the thoughts come
unbidden, but welcome for once.
Every pencil scratch is a whisper,
"Welcome back, welcome back."
"You are home."